Stories
from the
Bible

ARCTURUS

ARCTURUS

This edition published in 2017 by Arcturus Publishing Limited
26/27 Bickels Yard, 151–153 Bermondsey Street,
London SE1 3HA

Copyright © Arcturus Holdings Limited

ISBN: 978-1-78428-681-1
CH005662NT
Supplier 26, Date 0717, Print run 6248

Written and adapted by Alex Woolf
Illustrated by Natalie Hinrichsen
Edited by Susannah Bailey
Designed by Elaine Wilkinson

Printed in China

Introduction

This book contains brand new retellings of some of the most popular stories from the Bible. The Bible is a collection of holy books. These books were written over many hundreds of years by lots of authors who were guided and inspired by God.

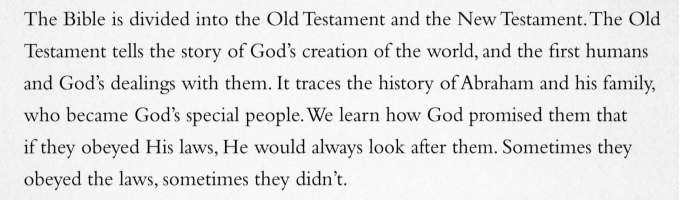

The Bible is divided into the Old Testament and the New Testament. The Old Testament tells the story of God's creation of the world, and the first humans and God's dealings with them. It traces the history of Abraham and his family, who became God's special people. We learn how God promised them that if they obeyed His laws, He would always look after them. Sometimes they obeyed the laws, sometimes they didn't.

The New Testament is the story of Jesus, the son of God, and his message of love and forgiveness for the people of the world. This book includes some of the best-loved stories about Jesus, such as his birth, how he found his disciples, the incredible miracles he performed, the people he helped, and the wise parables he told. Finally, we hear the sad, yet uplifting, story of his death and resurrection.

The stories in this collection have been specially selected for their appeal to children. They feature dramatic storylines and strong, simple messages. We hope you enjoy them!

The Old Testament

The New Testament

The Old Testament

How God Created the World

Long ago, before the world was created, there was nothing but darkness. Then God said, "Let there be light," and there was light! God called the light "day" and the darkness "night," and that was the first day.

On the second day, God created the sky. He called it "Heaven." Under the sky, there was nothing but water. On day three, God made the land, which He called "Earth." He made the Earth grow grass and plants and trees with fruit.

God created the Sun, the Moon, and the stars on the fourth day. He made the Sun shine in the daytime and the Moon and stars shine at night. On the fifth day, He created all the birds that fill the sky and all the fish that swim in the seas.

On the sixth day, God made the animals that live on the land. He created the first man, whose name was Adam. He blessed him and told him to look after all the creatures He had made.

God made the seventh day a holy day, and said it should always be a time of rest.

Adam and Eve

God planted a beautiful garden in a place on Earth called Eden. He told Adam he could eat the fruit of every tree except one. That was the Tree of Knowledge, which was in the middle of the garden. "If you eat the fruit from that tree, you will die," God warned him. Adam liked living in the Garden of Eden, but he was lonely. So God gave him a wife and named her Eve.

Now, in the garden, there lived a cunning serpent. One day, the serpent spoke to Eve. "Did God say you could eat the fruit from all the trees in this garden?" he asked. Eve replied, "All except the one in the middle. He said we would die if we ate from it." The serpent hissed, "You won't die, Eve. You will become wise."

The fruit hanging from the Tree of Knowledge looked delicious, so Eve picked one and bit into it. It was delicious. She gave half of it to Adam, and he ate it, too. Then Adam and Eve looked at each other and saw for the first time that they were naked. So they sewed leaves together to cover themselves.

That evening, God called to Adam, and Adam hid because he was ashamed. "Did you eat the fruit I told you not to eat?" God asked. "Eve gave it to me," said Adam. "Why did you disobey me?" God asked Eve. "The serpent told me to," said Eve.

God was angry with Adam and Eve for disobeying Him, and He drove them out of the Garden of Eden. "From now on," He said, "you will have to work hard to grow food. The ground will be hard and full of thorns and thistles. And when you become old, you will die."

Noah and the Ark

After many years, God looked at the world He had made, and He was sad. The people had become wicked. There was only one man who still loved and obeyed God, and his name was Noah. God said to Noah: "I am going to destroy the world in a giant flood, but you and your family will be spared."

He told Noah to build a huge boat called an ark, strong enough to survive the flood. Noah had to take two of every creature aboard the ark, so that they would also be saved. Noah did as God commanded, and after many months of hard work, the ark was finally finished. As Noah and his family loaded the animals and the food onto the ark, dark clouds began to gather.

Then the rain began to fall. It rained and it rained. Soon the rivers started to swell, and the land became flooded. The water began to rise, and the ark rose with it. For forty days and forty nights, the rain continued to fall. The entire world was covered in water, even the tops of mountains. The ark was rocked by stormy waves, but it stayed afloat, and those on board remained safe and dry.

At last, the rain stopped, and the water began to go down. Noah sent a raven in search of dry land. But the raven could not find any, so Noah sent a dove. The dove came back with an olive leaf in its beak. Now Noah knew the floodwaters were coming down.

Everyone was so happy when they reached the land that they rushed out of the ark. Noah thanked God for saving them from the flood. God promised Noah He would never again flood the world. He put a rainbow in the sky to remind people of His promise.

The Tower of Babel

Many more years passed, and Noah's children had children of their own. And those children had children. The world began to fill up with people again. And all people spoke the same language.

The people decided they needed to find new lands to settle. So they moved eastward until they came to a place called Shinar, where they stopped and built the city of Babel. "Let's build a tower in the middle of the city," the people said. "Let's build it so high, it reaches all the way up to Heaven." So they set to work building their tower.

God saw what they were doing, and He was not pleased. Heaven was a holy place that could not be entered by building a tower. God decided He had to stop people from plotting together to bring disaster on the world. So He scattered the people of Babel across the face of the Earth. And He made them speak different languages, so that they could no longer understand each other.

As for the Tower of Babel, it remained unfinished, and in time, it crumbled to dust.

Abraham and Sarah

Abraham was a wealthy man who lived in Mesopotamia with his wife, Sarah. They were both old and very sad that they had not been blessed with children.

One day, God spoke to Abraham. He told him to journey to the land of Canaan, where God would make Abraham the father of a great nation. This was difficult for Abraham, who would have to give up his comfortable life in Mesopotamia to go and live in a tent in a faraway land. But Abraham trusted God, and so he obeyed Him.

He and Sarah set out on the journey with their servants and their herds of sheep and goats. At last, they arrived in Canaan, where they set up their tent. Life was hard in Canaan, but again, God promised Abraham that he would be the father of a great nation.

Several years later, one hot afternoon, Abraham was visited by three men. He welcomed them, offering them food and water. While they were eating, one of the men said to Abraham, "In nine months, Sarah, your wife, will have a son."

Sarah was watching them from the entrance of her tent. She laughed when she heard this. She told the man that she was far too old to have a son. Then the man said, "Why do you laugh? Is anything too hard for God? You shall have a son, and he shall be named Isaac." When he heard these words, Abraham realized that these were not ordinary men. They spoke the words of God.

God kept His promise, and nine months later, Sarah gave birth to a son. She was so happy that she laughed for joy. And, of course, she and Abraham named him Isaac.

Isaac and Rebecca

Isaac grew into a tall and handsome young man. One day, Abraham decided it was time for his son to get married. Abraham wanted the the chosen girl to come from the land of his people, so he sent a servant to Mesopotamia to find Isaac a wife.

The servant journeyed there with ten of his master's camels and gifts for the girl and her family. After a long journey, the servant arrived at the city of Abraham's birth. He stopped at a well outside the city.

Here he kneeled down and prayed to God, saying, "Please help me find Isaac a wife. When the girls come to the well to fill their jars, I will ask one of them for water. If she gives me water and offers water to my camels, let her be a wife for Isaac."

When the servant opened his eyes, he saw a beautiful girl approaching. He asked her for water, and she gave some to him and some to his camels as well. The servant was overjoyed. His prayer had been answered! "What is your name?" he asked her. "Rebecca," she replied. "I am the granddaughter of Nahor."

Nahor was Abraham's brother. The servant thanked God for leading him to Abraham's family. He gave Rebecca gifts from Abraham and explained why he had come. Rebecca took the servant home and repeated his story to her family. They understood that God wanted Rebecca to go to Canaan and marry Isaac.

After saying goodbye to her family, Rebecca went to Canaan with the servant. Isaac was out in the fields when he saw the camels approaching. He went to meet them, and the servant told him all that had happened. When Isaac and Rebecca saw each other, they immediately fell in love.

Jacob and Esau

Isaac and Rebecca had twin sons named Esau and Jacob. Esau was the older twin, which meant that he would become head of the family when Isaac died. This was his "birthright." Esau grew up to be a hairy man who loved to hunt. Jacob, who was Rebecca's dearest son, preferred to stay in his tent.

One day, Esau returned from his hunt feeling very hungry. He said to Jacob, "Give me some stew, brother, or I shall starve." Jacob said, "First give me your birthright." So Esau gave Jacob his birthright in return for some stew.

Isaac grew older, and his eyesight became weak. One day he called Esau to his bedside and said, "My son, I will die soon. Go out and hunt me a deer, so I can eat its meat. Then I will give you my blessing, and you shall become head of the family." So Esau went to hunt.

Rebecca overheard this conversation. She wanted Jacob to become head of the family instead, so she formed a plan to deceive Isaac. After preparing a dish of goat meat, she said to Jacob, "Take this to your father. He will think you are Esau and give you his blessing." Rebecca gave Jacob Esau's cloak, and she covered his arms and neck with goatskin, which was hairy, like Esau.

"Who brings me this food?" asked Isaac, when Jacob came into his tent. "It is your son, Esau," said Jacob. "You sound like Jacob," said Isaac. "Come closer." So Jacob came closer. Isaac smelled the cloak, and he felt the hairy hands. Now he was sure it was Esau, and he gave him his blessing.

When Esau returned from the hunt, he was shocked to hear that Jacob had been blessed instead of him. "Bless me, too, Father!" he begged, but Isaac said it was too late. Jacob was now head of the family.

Joseph and His Special Coat

Jacob had twelve sons, but the one he treasured most was Joseph. To show how much he loved him, Jacob made Joseph a splendid coat. Joseph's brothers saw him walking around in his beautiful coat, and they were jealous.

One day, Joseph had a dream. He told his brothers: "I dreamed that the sun, the moon, and the eleven stars all bowed down to me." Now, the brothers hated Joseph even more. Even his father was cross. "What does this mean?" he cried. "Shall your mother and I and all your brothers, bow down to you?"

Joseph's brothers were so angry that they plotted against him. One day, when they were out feeding their flock, Joseph came to them. They stripped him of his magnificent coat and threw him into a pit. Just then, some merchants passed by on their way to Egypt. The brothers sold Joseph to the merchants as a slave.

The brothers killed a goat and dipped Joseph's coat in its blood. They took the bloodstained coat to their father and told him that a wild beast had eaten Joseph. Jacob was heartbroken. His wife and sons tried to cheer him up, but Jacob refused to be comforted.

Joseph in Egypt

When the merchants arrived in Egypt, they sold Joseph to an important man named Potiphar. Joseph worked hard for his new master, and Potiphar was so pleased with him that he put him in charge of his household.

Now Joseph was a handsome young man, and Potiphar's wife fell in love with him. She begged Joseph to love her, too, but Joseph refused, because it would mean betraying his master. Potiphar's wife took her revenge and told her husband that Joseph had mocked her. This was not true, but Potiphar was angry with Joseph and put him in prison.

While Joseph was in prison, he met a butler and a baker. They told Joseph their dreams. Joseph explained what the dreams meant, and the men were impressed. After the butler was freed from prison, he went to work for Pharaoh, the king of Egypt. One night, Pharaoh had a dream. In his dream, seven fat cows came out of the river, and they fed in the meadow. Then seven thin cows came out of the river and ate up the seven fat cows.

Pharaoh asked if there was anyone in the kingdom who could explain his dream. The butler said that Joseph could. So Pharaoh ordered that Joseph be released from prison and brought before him. Pharaoh told Joseph his dream. "The seven fat cows are seven years of good harvests when there will be plenty of food. The seven thin cows are seven years of poor harvests when there will be nothing to eat," Joseph said in response.

Pharaoh was so impressed, he made Joseph his governor and placed him in charge of Egypt. For the next seven years, the harvests were good, and Joseph ordered that the extra food be placed in storehouses. When the seven bad years came, Joseph opened up the storehouses and sold the food to the people.

Back in Canaan, Joseph's father and brothers were getting very hungry, so Jacob sent his sons to Egypt to buy food. When they reached Egypt, they bowed down before Joseph. They did not know who he was, but Joseph recognized his brothers. He wanted to test them to see if they had changed their wicked ways.

He invited his brothers to his house where they were served a magnificent feast. The next morning, the brothers started back to Canaan with sacks filled with grain. Suddenly, they were surrounded by soldiers. One soldier shouted at them, saying, "You have stolen the governor's silver cup!" The soldier searched their sacks. In the sack of the youngest brother, Benjamin, he found the cup. This was all part of Joseph's plan.

Joseph pretended to be angry. He threatened to make Benjamin his slave. But one of his other brothers pleaded with him, saying, "If you keep Benjamin, my father will die of grief. He has already lost his beloved son, Joseph. Please take me instead." Now, Joseph knew his brothers had changed. He told them: "I am Joseph, your long-lost brother. Go back to my father and bring him here, and we will all live happily in Egypt."

Moses in the Bulrushes

Jacob and his sons settled in Egypt. They became known as the children of Israel (Israel was God's name for Jacob), or Israelites. Many years passed, and the Israelites stayed in Egypt, and their numbers greatly increased.

By now, Egypt had a new pharaoh, who feared the Israelites' growing strength. He made them work as slaves, building new cities for him. But the Israelites continued to grow in number. "Every Israelite boy that is born must be cast into the river," Pharaoh told his soldiers.

One Israelite mother managed to hide her baby son. But as he grew older, she feared Pharaoh's soldiers would hear him crying. So she made a basket of reeds and put her baby in it. Then she took it to the river's edge and laid it among the bulrushes.

Later, Pharaoh's daughter came to the river to bathe. She spotted the baby in the basket. "That must be an Israelite boy," she said to her maid. The baby started crying, and the princess took pity on him. She decided to raise him as her own son. The princess named the boy Moses. He grew up in the royal palace and was treated like a prince, but he never forgot he was an Israelite.

One day, Moses saw an Egyptian whipping an Israelite slave. Moses killed the Egyptian. He knew that if Pharaoh heard about this, he would be put to death. So Moses fled into the desert.

While he was living in the desert, Moses saw a bush on fire, but it wasn't burning up. Astonished by this sight, Moses went closer. Then he heard God speaking to him. "Moses," said God. "Your people, the children of Israel, are miserable. You must lead them out of Egypt to Canaan, where they can be free."

Moses Leads His People to Freedom

As God had instructed, Moses went before Pharaoh and asked him to let the Israelites go. Pharaoh was angry at him for asking and refused to let them leave (in fact, he made them work even harder). So Moses went back to Pharaoh. He warned him that if he didn't let the Israelites go, God would bring terrible disasters upon Egypt.

Again, Pharaoh refused, and so the terrible disasters began. First, the Nile River turned red, and no one could drink from its waters. Then, thousands of frogs came swarming out of the river. The frogs got everywhere, even in Pharaoh's palace.

Next, God sent clouds of stinging, buzzing gnats and flies. Disease swept the land, killing animals and causing people to get sick. Each time disaster struck, Moses begged Pharaoh to change his mind, but Pharaoh always refused.

God raised a storm of giant hailstones. He sent swarms of locusts to devour Egypt's crops. Still Pharaoh refused to release the Israelites. Then God sent a final, terrible disaster, and one night, the firstborn son of every Egyptian family died.

At last, Pharaoh agreed to let the Israelites go. The next day, Moses led his people out of Egypt. But when they reached the shores of the Red Sea, they saw Egyptian soldiers chasing after them. Pharaoh had changed his mind.

Now the Israelites were trapped between the soldiers and the sea. They were scared, but Moses told them that God would save them. He held up his staff over the Red Sea, and the waters parted. The Israelites crossed a path through the sea to the other side. When the Egyptian soldiers tried to follow, the waters closed up over them, and they were swallowed by the sea.

The Ten Commandments

Moses led his people through the desert toward the promised land of Canaan. It was a long journey, and the people grew hungry. They complained to Moses, saying, "In Egypt, we had all the food we wanted. Now we're starving. Why did you lead us here?"

God heard their grumbling, and He said to Moses: "I will give them food." That evening, birds flew over the camp and came to rest on the ground. The people caught them and cooked them for their meat, and they were hungry no longer.

In the morning, the people woke to find small white seeds lying on the ground. They ground them into flour, which they made into cakes. The people called the seeds "manna." Each evening, more birds came, and each morning, manna fell from Heaven. So the Israelites always had enough to eat.

But then, they became thirsty. They complained to Moses, saying, "In Egypt, we had enough water to drink. Now we have none. Why did you lead us here?"

"What shall I do? The people might hurt me," Moses pleaded with God. "Go with your stick to a rock that I will show you. Strike the rock with your stick," God replied. Moses did as he was instructed, and when he struck the rock, fresh water gushed out for drinking. In this way, God looked after the Israelites during the time they lived in the desert. He sent them food and water.

Eventually, they arrived at the foot of Mount Sinai where they set up camp. Moses climbed the mountain to speak with God. God gave Moses ten commandments for the people to obey:

1. You must have no other gods but me.
2. You must not make images of any gods or worship them.
3. You must not say my name, except with respect.
4. Always remember the Sabbath day, and keep it holy.
5. Respect your father and your mother.
6. You must not kill.
7. Husbands and wives must be faithful to each other.
8. You must not steal.
9. You must not lie.
10. You must not envy others for the things they have.

Moses came back down the mountain and told the people God's commandments. The people promised to obey them. Then, Moses went back up the mountain to speak again with God. He did not return for a long time, and the people grew restless, so they built a golden calf and praised it.

Eventually, Moses returned to the camp. When he found the people glorifying the golden calf, he got very angry, because the people had broken the second of God's commandments.

Moses begged God to forgive the people. God told Moses to write down the commandments on tablets of stone. Then, God made the people promise once more to always obey His commandments. In return, He promised to always look after them.

The Battle of Jericho

The Israelites wandered the desert for forty years. Eventually, Moses died. The new leader of the Israelites was Joshua. It was his task to lead them into Canaan, the promised land. To reach Canaan, however, they had to cross the Jordan River.

After they had crossed the river, they came to the city of Jericho. They would have to capture Jericho before they could enter Canaan. But Jericho was well defended with huge stone walls.

The people of Jericho knew the Israelites were planning to attack, so they kept the gates shut, and no one entered or left the city.

God told Joshua how to capture Jericho. Then Joshua called the people to him and gave them their orders. Seven priests marched around the city carrying trumpets made from rams' horns. When Joshua gave the signal, all the people shouted, and the priests blew their horns. After that, they returned to their camp.

They did this for six days. On the seventh day, when the people shouted and the priests blew their horns, the walls of Jericho came crashing down. The Israelites entered the city and took control of it.

Samson and Delilah

Many years after they settled in Canaan, the Israelites were conquered by a people called the Philistines. Among the Israelites was a man named Manoah. He and his wife had no children. One day, an angel came to the couple and told them they were to have a son. When the boy grew up, he would save the Israelites from the Philistines. "But," the angel warned them, "you must never cut your son's hair."

In time, they had a son and named him Samson. He grew up big and strong. Samson fought the Philistines and killed a great number of them. Then Samson fell in love with a Philistine woman named Delilah. The Philistines promised Delilah a great reward if she could discover the secret of Samson's strength.

Delilah begged Samson to tell her, and Samson teased her with tales that weren't true. Eventually, Delilah said, "How can you say you love me if you will not tell me your secret?" So Samson gave in and replied, "If you cut my hair, I will lose my strength and become like other men."

Delilah waited for Samson to fall asleep, then she cut off his hair. When he awoke, the Philistines captured him. They blinded Samson and put him in prison. Gradually, his hair grew back, but they didn't notice. The Philistines held a big celebration in their temple to give thanks to their god. They brought Samson to the temple and chained him up between two pillars, and they mocked him.

Samson prayed to God for strength, so he could take revenge on the Philistines. Then he put his hands on the pillars and pushed with all his might! The pillars cracked, and the whole temple came crashing down, killing all the Philistine leaders and Samson himself. By doing this, Samson rescued the Israelites from the Philistines.

David and Goliath

In time, the Philistines grew strong again, and the Israelites had to fight them in a war. As the two armies faced each other, ready for battle, a Philistine came to see the Israelites. He was a giant more than ten feet tall, and his name was Goliath.

He said to the Israelites, "Choose a man to fight me. If he kills me, you win the war. But if I kill him, we win." The Israelites didn't know what to do. There was no one among them with the strength to defeat Goliath.

Then a shepherd boy named David went to see Saul, king of the Israelites. "I will fight Goliath," he said. "But you are just a shepherd boy," replied Saul. And David said, "With God's help, I once killed a lion that attacked my sheep. God will help me now."

So Saul let David fight Goliath. David walked out to meet Goliath armed only with a slingshot. When Goliath saw David, he laughed and said, "Come here, boy. I will kill you." David swung his weapon and fired a stone at Goliath. It struck him on his forehead, and Goliath fell down dead. When the Philistines saw this, they ran.

Wise King Solomon

David grew up to become king of Israel. After he died, his son Solomon became king. He was only a teenager when he came to the throne. One night, the king had a dream in which God asked him: "Solomon, what would you like me to give you?" Solomon replied, "Oh God, I am very young and don't yet know how to be a good king. Please give me wisdom, so that I can rule my people well."

God was very pleased with this answer. "You could have asked for riches and glory. Instead, you asked for wisdom. For that reason, I will make you the wisest man who ever lived. And I will give you riches and glory," He said.

As Solomon grew older, he became known far and wide for his great wisdom. One day, two women came before him with a difficult problem. One of them was carrying a baby. The other woman explained, "This woman and I live in the same house. I gave birth to a baby boy, and a few days later, so did she. Her baby died, so she stole mine."

"No, it was your baby who died," said the first woman. "This baby is mine." Solomon sent for his sword. When the sword arrived, Solomon ordered a guard to cut the baby in two, then give each woman half of it.

"No!" screamed the first woman. "Please don't kill the baby. Give it to her." Now Solomon knew that this was the real mother. She loved the baby so much that she was willing to give him to the other woman, so that he wouldn't be killed. Solomon handed the baby to the first woman.

Elijah

Many years after the reign of Solomon, Israel was ruled by a king named Ahab. He turned away from God and praised another god, Baal. A holy man named Elijah begged Ahab not to worship Baal. He warned that there would be no rain for many years, and the people would starve. This made Ahab angry at Elijah. God told Elijah to flee the city and go and live in a distant valley.

Then, the drought came, and the people of Israel suffered. After three years, Elijah returned to Ahab. "Tell the people of Israel and all the prophets of Baal to come to the top of Mount Carmel. Then we shall see who is the true God," he said to the king.

So they all went up Mount Carmel. "Build an altar, and call on Baal to set it on fire," Elijah challenged the prophets. The prophets did as Elijah asked. They prayed for fire, but no fire came.

Then Elijah built an altar. He poured water on it to make it harder to burn. He prayed to God, and immediately, the altar burst into flames. The people watching were amazed. They fell on their knees and cried, "The Lord, he is the true God."

Daniel in the Lions' Den

Long after the time of Elijah, the city of Jerusalem in Israel was attacked by the Babylonians. The Israelites, now also known as Jews, were taken as captives to Babylon. Some young Jewish boys were chosen to become members of the king's household. Among them was a handsome, intelligent boy named Daniel.

As Daniel grew up, he impressed the king with his wisdom. The king made him a chief advisor and put him in charge of all the princes in the kingdom. But Daniel never forgot that he was a Jew, and he prayed to God three times a day.

Some of the princes were jealous of Daniel and wanted to get rid of him. They tried to find something that he had done wrong but could find nothing. Finally, they went to the king and said, "Oh King, you should pass a new law. For thirty days, no one must pray to any god but you. If anyone prays to another god, they should be thrown into a den of lions."

The king passed the law. Then the princes went to Daniel's house and saw him praying to God. They told the king that Daniel had broken his law. The king was sad because he loved Daniel, but the law was the law. So Daniel was taken from his house and cast into the lions' den.

All that night, the king couldn't sleep. Early the next morning, he hurried to the lions' den and called out: "Daniel, did your god save you?" Daniel replied, "Yes, oh King, I am still alive. God closed the lions' mouths so they would not hurt me."

The king was very happy to hear this. He released Daniel and ordered the princes who accused him to be put into the lions' den. Then he passed a law that the God of Daniel should be respected in his kingdom.

Esther Saves Her People

Babylonia was eventually conquered by Persia. The Jews were allowed to return to Israel, but many remained in Babylonia. Among those who remained was a man named Mordecai and his beautiful young cousin, Esther.

When the king of Persia saw Esther, he fell in love with her. "This girl will be my new queen," he announced. Mordecai was given a job in the royal household, so the cousins remained in touch.

The king had a prime minister named Haman. He was a proud man and insisted that everyone bow down to him. Mordecai refused to bow. "I am a Jew," he explained, "and I only bow to God." Haman was furious. He decided to punish not only Mordecai but all the Jews. He went to the king and said, "Your Majesty, there are some people in your kingdom who are disobeying your laws. Can I punish them?"

The king said he could. Haman then ordered that all the Jews should be killed on a certain day. Mordecai was horrified. He asked Esther for help. Esther went to the king and asked him if he and Haman would dine with her. So that evening, the king and Haman came to dinner. While they were eating, Esther asked the king if he would do something for her. "Of course, my queen," he replied. "I'll do anything you ask."

"I ask only that you save my life and the life of my people, for we are soon to be put to death," said Esther. "Who would dare to give such an order?" thundered the king. Esther pointed to Haman. The prime minister turned pale with fear. He had not realized that Esther was a Jew. The king ordered Haman to be hanged. In this way, Queen Esther saved her people.

Jonah and the Whale

Once there was a man named Jonah who lived in the land of Israel. One day, God spoke to him. God told him to go to the city of Nineveh and tell the people there to stop being so wicked. Jonah, however, did not want to go to Nineveh or to help the people there. He wanted God to punish them for being bad. So Jonah got on a ship that was sailing to another city. God wasn't happy with Jonah for running away, and so He caused a huge storm.

Jonah knew that God had caused the storm because He was angry with him. He told the sailors to throw him overboard. As soon as Jonah fell into the sea, the storm stopped, and the sea became calm.

God didn't want Jonah to drown, so He sent a huge whale to swallow him. For three days and three nights, Jonah lived inside the whale and prayed to God to forgive him. Finally, the whale spat Jonah out. Jonah decided he had no choice but to do what God had asked. He went to Nineveh and told the people there to stop being so cruel and wicked. The people listened to him. They prayed to God and were sorry for being bad, and God forgave them.

The New Testament

An Angel Appears to Mary

Mary was a young woman who lived in the village of Nazareth in Judea. She was engaged to be married to Joseph, the local carpenter. One day, she was sitting outside her house when a strange light fell upon her.

She looked up and was astonished to see the angel Gabriel standing there. "Don't be frightened, Mary," said Gabriel. "God is with you. I come with good news. You are going to have a son. You will call him Jesus. He is the long-awaited king whose kingdom will last forever."

"How can this happen?" asked Mary. "I'm not yet married." Gabriel answered: "God is with you, and your child will be God's own son." Mary was confused, but she said: "I am God's servant, and I will do whatever He asks of me."

After the angel had gone, Mary decided to visit her cousin Elizabeth, the only person Mary felt she could talk to about this. When she arrived at Elizabeth's house, the cousins greeted each other warmly.

To Mary's amazement, Elizabeth said that she, too, had been visited by the angel Gabriel, and she was due to have a baby in three months. His name would be John, and he would do great things.

Joseph the carpenter was looking forward to marrying Mary. When he discovered she was going to have a child, he was very upset. He thought another man must be the father, and he decided that because of this he could no longer marry her.

That night, however, God spoke to Joseph in a dream. "Don't worry, Joseph," said God. "Mary's baby will be born through God's Holy Spirit. Marry her, and bring the child up as your own." When Joseph awoke, he felt much happier and began making plans for their wedding.

The Birth of Jesus

Mary and Joseph lived in Judea, which was part of the Roman Empire. The Roman emperor passed a law stating that all men had to go to the town of their birth and register, so they could be taxed. So Joseph had to travel to Bethlehem, where he grew up. He took his new wife Mary with him, even though she was soon to have her baby.

When they arrived in Bethlehem, there was no room at the inn, so they had to sleep in the stable. That night, the baby was born. Mary and Joseph gazed happily at the tiny boy. "We'll name him Jesus," said Mary, "as the angel told me." She wrapped him in swaddling clothes. Since they had no cradle, they laid him in a manger.

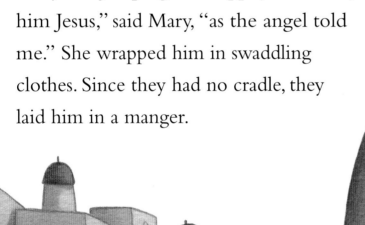

Meanwhile, in a nearby field, shepherds watched over their sheep. Suddenly, the sky lit up, and an angel appeared. "I bring good news. This night, a baby was born in Bethlehem. He is Christ the Lord. You will find him wrapped in swaddling clothes and lying in a manger," the angel said.

The angel vanished, and the astonished shepherds ran to Bethlehem to see if it was true. When they found the baby lying in the manger, they fell on their knees and praised him.

The Three Wise Men

In a land far to the east of Bethlehem, three wise men were studying the stars. One night, they saw a bright new star and knew this was a sign that a great king had been born. They decided to follow the star as it moved through the night sky.

At last, they reached Jerusalem, capital of Judea, and asked if a new king had been born. When Herod, king of the Jews, heard about this, he was worried. The Roman rulers of Judea had made Herod king, and he didn't want a new king taking his throne. He asked his priests about it. They studied their old books and found a prophesy that the king of the Jews would be born in Bethlehem.

Herod said to the wise men, "The new king has been born in Bethlehem. When you find him, come back and tell me where he is, so I can visit him with gifts of my own."

The wise men found Mary, Joseph, and Jesus living quietly in Bethlehem. They offered the infant king gifts of gold, frankincense, and myrrh.

That night, God warned the wise men not to return to Herod. So the next morning, they started back to their homeland by a different route.

That same night, God spoke to Joseph in a dream. He said: "Jesus is in danger. King Herod is sending his soldiers to Bethlehem with orders to kill the baby. Go to Egypt where you will be safe." Joseph woke Mary. They quickly started packing up their things.

Herod was angry when the wise men didn't return. He ordered his soldiers to go to Bethlehem and kill every boy under two years old. The people of Bethlehem cursed Herod for his cruelty. But the soldiers didn't find Jesus. By this time, he and his parents were safely on their way to Egypt.

Jesus in the Temple

In time, Herod died, and it became safe for Joseph, Mary, and Jesus to return to Nazareth. Years passed, and Jesus grew into a determined, curious child. When he was twelve years old, Mary and Joseph took him to Jerusalem for the festival of Passover. This celebrated the time when Moses led the Jews to freedom from slavery in Egypt.

When the festival was over, the family started back to Nazareth. At the end of the first day, Mary and Joseph noticed that Jesus wasn't with them. They asked other members of the group they were walking with where he was, but no one had seen him.

The worried parents returned to Jerusalem. They searched the city for three days but couldn't find him anywhere. Finally, someone said he'd seen Jesus in the Temple. So Mary and Joseph hurried to the Temple. Here, they found him sitting among the teachers, listening to them and asking them questions. The teachers were astonished that someone this young could be so wise.

Mary ran to Jesus and took him roughly by the arm. "My son, why did you come here without telling us? Your father and I have been searching everywhere for you. We were so worried!" Jesus replied, "I am sorry, Mother. But did you not know that you would find me in my Father's house?"

Mary and Joseph took Jesus back to Nazareth. The years passed, and Jesus grew into a strong and wise young man who loved his parents and God. Mary often wondered about what she had witnessed that day in the Temple. She knew her son was special, but did not know yet what God intended for him.

John Baptizes Jesus

Mary's cousin, Elizabeth, had a son named John. As a young man, the spirit of God entered him. He went out into the desert around Jordan, dressed in rough clothing, and ate locusts and wild honey.

People soon came to listen to John preach. He told them that God's kingdom was on its way and urged them to confess their sins. He washed their sins clean by baptizing them in the Jordan River.

"There is someone coming whose shoes I am not worthy to undo. I baptize you with water, but he will baptize you with the Holy Spirit and with fire," John told the crowds.

One day, Jesus came to Jordan to be baptized by John. When John saw who he was, he said, "Why do you come to me to be baptized? I should be baptized by you." Jesus replied, "This is what God wants." After John had baptized Jesus, a dove flew down and landed on Jesus, and God said, "This is my beloved son. I am most pleased with him."

The Twelve Disciples

When Jesus was about thirty years old, he began to preach. He told people that God's kingdom was coming, and they should ask forgiveness for their sins. Wherever he went, Jesus attracted crowds of people eager to hear his message.

One day, Jesus was walking along the shore of Lake Galilee when he saw two fishermen named Peter and Andrew. He asked them if they

could take him out on their boat. So they rowed him out onto the lake a little way, and he stood up and spoke to the people watching him from the shore.

When he had finished speaking, Jesus asked Peter and Andrew to row farther out and let down their nets to catch some fish. "We've been fishing all night and have caught nothing," Peter told Jesus. But when they did as he asked, they caught so many fish, their nets broke.

Peter and Andrew called to their friends, John and James, to come and help. John and James came out in their own boat. Between them, the four men caught such a big haul of fish, it nearly sank their boats. They fell at Jesus' feet in amazement. "Follow me, and I will make you fishers of men," Jesus told them. The men immediately put aside their nets and followed him. They were Jesus' first disciples.

Jesus continued on his way, and he found more disciples. There were twelve altogether. The other disciples were Philip, Bartholomew, Matthew, Thomas, James (son of Alphaeus), Thaddaeus, Simon, and Judas. These were Jesus' special friends and followers. They went everywhere with him, listening to his teachings and helping to spread his message.

Jesus Heals the Sick

Jesus journeyed from place to place with his disciples, and there were always lots of people who wanted to hear him preach. He then began to perform miracles. At a wedding in Cana Jesus turned water into wine, and in a synagogue in Capernaum he healed a man possessed with a bad spirit.

Soon, people suffering from sickness or disease came to Jesus to be healed by him. His fame spread, and wherever he went, there was always a crowd surrounding him.

One day, Jesus was preaching in someone's house when some men arrived. They were carrying a paralyzed man in a bed, and they hoped Jesus would heal him. But they couldn't get into the house because it was so crowded. So the men climbed up the wall and lowered the man through the roof into the room where Jesus was.

Jesus saw the faith these men had, and he said to the paralyzed man, "Your sins are forgiven." Some religious leaders were in the room, and when they heard Jesus say this, they were angry. "Who can forgive sins, apart from God?" they cried. So Jesus asked them, "Is it easier to forgive this man his sins or to make him walk again? Let me show you that I have the power to forgive sins."

Then Jesus turned to the paralyzed man. "Arise. Take up your bed, and go back to your house," he said. Immediately, the man got up and carried his bed back to his house, praising God as he went. Everyone in the room was amazed and also a little frightened. They had never seen anything like this before.

The Sermon on the Mount

The Jewish leaders at that time believed that the only way to please God was to follow the laws that Moses had given. But Jesus said that simply obeying the laws wasn't enough, since it's what is inside peoples' hearts that matters most to God.

One day, Jesus walked up a mountain. He found a place where he could be seen by all those who had come to listen to him. Then he started to speak, saying, "Blessed are the poor in spirit, for theirs is the kingdom of Heaven." This meant that people who are not attached to their possessions and who share what they own with others, will find God.

"If we are humble and not easily angered, we will be rewarded. We must always try our best to do the right thing, even if we are punished for it. Although we might often fail, we should keep trying to do good. We should be kind and loving to others, and help people get along with each other."

Jesus said this and many other wise things that day in his Sermon on the Mount.

Jesus Calms the Storm

Jesus felt tired. He'd had a long day teaching and healing people on the shore of Lake Galilee. "Let us cross the lake," he said to his disciples. So they all climbed into their boat and prepared to set sail. Jesus rested his head on a cushion and instantly fell asleep.

While he slept, the wind began to howl, and the waves rose up, spilling over the sides of the boat. The disciples grew scared. They tried to scoop the water out of the boat, but however fast they did so, more water kept pouring in. Soon, they were sure the boat would sink.

They turned to Jesus and were astonished to see that he was still fast asleep. "Wake up!" they cried. "We are going to drown!" Jesus awoke. He stood up and spoke to the wind and waves. "Be still!" he commanded.

At once, the wind died, and the lake became calm. Then Jesus turned to his disciples. "Why were you frightened?" he asked them. "Did you not trust me?" The disciples were too shocked to answer. They whispered to each other, "What kind of man can make even the wind and waves obey him?"

Jairus' Daughter

Jairus was the leader of the synagogue and a very important man. One day, while Jesus was speaking to a crowd, Jairus came to him. "Please come quickly," he pleaded. "My daughter is very ill. She will die soon."

So Jesus followed Jairus toward his house, and the crowd continued to cluster around him as he walked. Suddenly, Jesus stopped. "Who touched me?" he asked. The disciples were surprised by the question. In such a crowd, it could have been anyone.

Eventually, a small, frail woman stepped forward and knelt at Jesus' feet. "I touched you," she said. "I have been ill for twelve years, and no doctor could cure me. I thought if I could touch your cloak, I might be cured, and so I was!" Jesus smiled warmly at her. In God's eyes, she was just as important as Jairus. "Your faith in me has made you well," he told her. "Go now, and enjoy a long, healthy life." So she made her way home, her heart filled with gratitude.

Meanwhile, Jairus was waiting impatiently for Jesus to come with him. Before they could continue, some people arrived with sad news: "Jairus, your daughter has died," they told him. "There is no point in bothering Jesus now." Jairus was heartbroken. If Jesus hadn't stopped to help that woman, his daughter might have been saved. But Jesus said to him, "Do not despair, Jairus. Your daughter is only sleeping."

He and Jairus hurried toward the house and entered the girl's room. Jesus took her hand. "Arise, little one," he said. Jairus's daughter immediately opened her eyes and rose from her bed. Her parents were filled with joy. They thanked Jesus, and he asked them not to tell anyone about it. "Simply give her something to eat," he said. Then, he walked quietly out of the house.

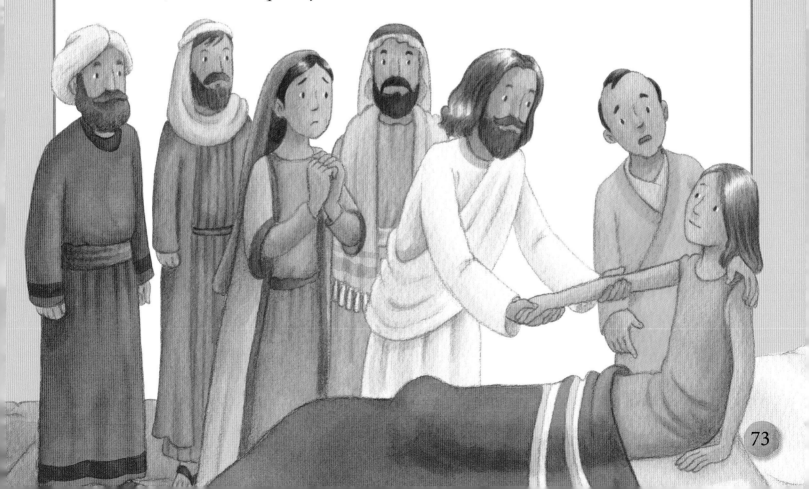

The Feeding of the Five Thousand

Jesus and his disciples needed to rest, so they sailed to a quiet spot on the shore of a lake. When they got there, however, they found a large crowd waiting for them. In the evening, the disciples said to Jesus, "Send the people away. We don't have enough food for them."

"Can't we give them a meal?" Jesus asked. "How?" cried the disciples. Then Andrew, one of the disciples, said, "There's a boy here who is offering his lunch. But it's only five loaves and two small fishes. What is that among so many?"

"Make everyone sit down," Jesus replied. He thanked the boy for offering his lunch. Then he broke the loaves and fishes into pieces and handed them to the disciples to give out to the crowd. Somehow, there was more than enough food to feed everyone. When everyone was full, Jesus told the disciples to gather up all the food that remained. They gathered it up and were amazed. Somehow, there was enough leftover food to fill twelve baskets.

Jesus Walks on Water

After the enormous picnic was over, the crowd went home. Jesus asked his disciples to get into their boat and head back across the lake. Then he went up into the mountains to pray.

While the disciples were on the lake, a fierce wind picked up. The wind was against them, and however hard they rowed, they couldn't move forward. Then they saw a shadowy figure approaching them. The figure was walking on the water as if it were solid ground. They trembled in fear, thinking it was a ghost.

But it wasn't a ghost, it was Jesus! "Do not be afraid," he called to them. "It is I." And Peter said, "If it is you, Lord, then let me come and join you." He stepped out of the boat and began walking toward Jesus on the water.

The wind blew harder, and Peter became scared. He started to sink. "Lord, save me!" he cried. Jesus held out his hand and caught Peter. "Why did you doubt me?" Jesus said. Jesus and Peter then climbed back onto the boat, and the wind immediately ceased. The disciples, witnessing all of this, cried, "Truly you are the Son of God!"

The Good Samaritan

One day, while Jesus was teaching, a lawyer stood up and asked him a question. "Master," he said, "I know that I must love my friend as I love myself, but who is my friend?"

Jesus answered him with a story, which went as follows. "There was once a Jew who went on a journey from Jerusalem to Jericho. On this journey, he was attacked by thieves. They beat him, stole his clothes and his money, and left him half dead by the side of the road.

"Later, a priest from the Temple in Jerusalem came by. When he saw the Jew lying there, he walked quickly past him on the other side of the road. Not long after that, another man who worked in the temple came along. He also noticed the Jew, and he, too, passed on by.

"Then there came a Samaritan walking along that road. Samaritans and Jews do not get along. But when this man saw the Jew, he felt pity for him. He got off his donkey and kneeled by his side. He poured oil on his wounds to soothe the pain and gave him wine to drink.

After bandaging him up, he helped the Jew onto his donkey and led him to an inn where he could rest.

"The next day, before the Samaritan departed, he gave the innkeeper some money and said to him, 'Take care of this man, and any extra money you spend, I will repay you when I come again.'"

"Which of these three men, do you think, was a friend to the Jew who was attacked by thieves?" Jesus asked the lawyer. "The Samaritan, because he showed mercy to him," the lawyer said. Jesus nodded and replied, "Go, and do likewise."

The Prodigal Son

Some religious leaders were watching Jesus talking to the crowd.
"Why does he talk and eat with sinners?" they complained.
Jesus heard them, and he said, "God loves everyone, good and bad.
If just one sinner is sorry for what he's done, God is happy."
Then he told them this to show this.

"There was a man with two sons. One day, the younger son said
to his father, 'Father, one day, half of all you own will be mine.
Please give it to me now.' So the father gave him his share, and the
younger son went away and wasted his money on a life of pleasure.
When all his money was gone,
he fell into poverty.

"The son thought to himself,
'I must go back to my
father and tell him I
have sinned. I am no
longer worthy of being

called his son. I'll ask him to make me one of his servants.' So the son returned to his father. But when he was still some way off, his father saw him looking thin and dressed in rags. He ran to his son and embraced him. He dressed him in a fine robe and put shoes on his feet, and he said, 'Tonight we shall eat, drink, and be merry.'

"When the elder son heard about this, he was angry. He said, 'Father, for all these years I've served you faithfully, yet you never threw a party for me. But when my brother returns after spending all your wealth, you do this for him.' The father replied, 'Son, you are always with me, and what I have is yours. But now, we should celebrate. Your brother was dead, and now he's alive. He was lost and now is found.'"

Mary, Martha, and Lazarus

Mary and Martha were sisters. They lived in Bethany, near Jerusalem, with their brother Lazarus. Jesus was good friends with them and would often stay at their house. One day, while Jesus was in the north, he received word that Lazarus was sick. Instead of rushing to help him, Jesus remained two more days where he was.

As Jesus and his disciples started south, he turned to them and said, "Lazarus is dead. And I'm glad for your sakes that I wasn't there to save him. What I'm going to do now will make you all believe in me." When they arrived in Bethany, they learned that Lazarus had been dead for four days. Mary and Martha were weighed down with sorrow. Martha said, "Lord, if you had been here, I know my brother would not have died." Jesus told her, "He that believes in me, though he is dead, shall live."

They went to his tomb, and Jesus told them to move aside the stone covering the entrance. He cried out in a loud voice: "Lazarus, come out!" A tense silence followed. Then, Lazarus came out of the tomb. He was still wrapped in his grave clothes, but he was alive and well.

Jesus Enters Jerusalem

The time of Passover was near, and Jesus and his disciples went to Jerusalem for the celebrations. Jesus rode into Jerusalem on a donkey with his disciples walking by his side. A huge crowd greeted him, for word had spread of his extraordinary miracles. The people laid a carpet of cloaks and palm leaves on the road before him. They sang, "Blessed be the king that comes in the name of the Lord."

The chief priests of the Temple were disturbed by this sight. They said to Jesus, "Tell your followers to be quiet." To this, Jesus replied, "If they were quiet, the stones themselves would sing out."

Jesus went into the Temple. It was full of people buying and selling animals and changing money. Jesus was very angry to see the Temple used like this. He pushed over the tables and drove the traders out, crying, "This should be a house of prayer, but you have made it a den of thieves." Jesus returned to the Temple the next day, and he taught the people about God and healed the sick.

The chief priests were worried that Jesus was becoming too popular. He was threatening their power, so they decided to get rid of him. But how? They didn't dare arrest him in the Temple because his followers might start a riot.

Then, Judas, one of the twelve disciples, came to them and said, "What will you give me if I deliver Jesus to you?" The chief priests promised to give him thirty pieces of silver. Judas agreed to this, and he began to look for a moment when he could betray Jesus to the chief priests. It would have to be a time when there were no crowds around.

The Last Supper

On the evening of Passover, the disciples gathered for supper. Jesus broke the bread into pieces and gave it to the disciples, saying, "This is my body. When you eat it, remember me." Then he poured them wine. "Drink this. It is my blood, which I have shed for you and many others," he said.

When the supper was over, Jesus kneeled before each disciple and washed their feet. "See how I, your Lord, wash your feet. You must do the same for each other. Be ready to serve each other as I have served you," he said.

Then, in a troubled voice, Jesus continued, "One of you here will betray me." The disciples were shocked. They looked at one other, wondering who Jesus could mean. "Lord, who is it?" one asked. Jesus replied, "It is he to whom I give this bread." And he dipped a piece of bread in water and handed it to Judas. "What you must do, do it quickly," Jesus said to him. Judas then ran out of the house.

Jesus turned to the others. "Soon, I must leave you. And where I am going, you cannot follow," he announced.

They went out of the city to a garden called Gethsemane. On the way, Jesus told the disciples that they would soon run away and leave him. They all promised that they wouldn't.

At Gethsemane, Jesus prayed to God for strength to cope with his coming ordeal. When he returned to his disciples, they were asleep. "Could you not stay awake with me, even for one hour?" he asked them. Twice Jesus woke them, but when he began to pray again, they dozed off.

Finally, he said to them, "Behold! He that betrays me is coming!" As he said this, Judas arrived, along with armed guards sent by the chief priests. Judas kissed Jesus, so that the guards would know who to arrest. The guards seized Jesus. In a fury, Peter drew his sword and cut off the ear of one of the guards. "Put down your sword!" Jesus told Peter, and he touched the man's ear, making it whole again.

The disciples were frightened, and they fled, just as Jesus had said they would. They left Jesus to be taken by the guards back to Jerusalem.

Jesus Dies on the Cross

Jesus was taken to the palace of Caiaphas, the high priest, where he was put on trial. Witnesses were called, but none could prove that Jesus had committed a crime. Finally, Caiaphas asked Jesus, "Are you the Son of God?" Jesus said he was. "To say that makes you guilty of a crime against God," declared Caiaphas.

The other religious leaders agreed that Jesus deserved to die for what he said. But they had no power to put a man to death. Only the Roman rulers of Judea could do that. So they took Jesus before Pontius Pilate, the Roman governor.

Pontius Pilate questioned Jesus but could find no law that he had broken. So Pilate went before the people and asked, "According to your custom, I should release one prisoner at Passover. Shall I release Jesus?"

The Jewish leaders persuaded the people to say no. Instead, they asked for the release of Barrabas, a robber and murderer. Pilate questioned them, saying, "What shall I do with Jesus?" And they replied, "Crucify him!" Pilate knew Jesus was innocent, but he didn't want to cause a riot. So he called for a bowl of water and washed his hands, to show that he was not to blame for Jesus' death.

Pilate ordered Jesus to be whipped. After they had whipped him, the soldiers mocked Jesus, dressing him up like a king with a robe and a crown made of thorns. Jesus was made to carry his cross up to a place called Golgotha, where he would be put to death.

The guards nailed Jesus' hands and feet to the cross. Then they raised it up between two other crosses. Jesus looked down at the jeering soldiers and said, "Forgive them Father, they don't know what they're doing." Jesus suffered on the cross for about six hours, until at three o'clock in the afternoon, he died.

Jesus Returns

Very early on Sunday morning, two days after Jesus died, some women went to visit his tomb. To their astonishment, the stone covering the entrance had been rolled aside, and the soldiers guarding the tomb had fled. Then an angel in white appeared before the women, saying: "Jesus has risen from the dead. Go and tell his disciples." Full of joy and excitement, the women ran to tell the disciples the news.

Later that day, two of the disciples were walking to a village called Emmaus, near Jerusalem. They were talking about the death of Jesus when a man approached them. They didn't realize that the man was Jesus. "Why do you look so sad?" he asked them. So they told him what had happened. When they reached Emmaus, they invited Jesus to stay and have supper with them.

When they sat down to eat, Jesus blessed the bread and broke it, giving each of them a piece. Suddenly, they knew that this man was Jesus. But at the same moment, Jesus vanished from sight. Quickly, the men returned to Jerusalem to tell the other disciples what they had witnessed.

As they were telling the others the news, Jesus appeared once again before them. The disciples were scared, thinking he was a ghost. But Jesus said, "Fear not. It is I, your Lord, standing before you. Touch me, and you will see that I am flesh and blood." They gave him food and watched him eat, and this convinced them that he was alive. "All this has been foretold by the prophets: Christ will die, and then rise again," Jesus explained.

One of the disciples, Thomas, wasn't there when Jesus appeared. Later, the other disciples told Thomas what had happened. But Thomas doubted their story. "Unless I see and touch the wounds in his hands and in his side, I won't believe Jesus has returned," he said.

Eight days later, Jesus appeared again before the disciples. This time, Thomas was with them, and Jesus said to him, "Touch the wounds in my hands and my side, Thomas. Then stop your doubting, and believe." Thomas replied: "I believe in you, my Lord." And Jesus said, "Because you have seen me, you believe in me. Blessed are they who have not seen me, yet still believe."

Jesus appeared a fourth time at the sea of Tiberias. Some of the disciples had been fishing all night and had caught nothing. In the morning, they saw Jesus standing on the shore, but they didn't know it was him. "Cast your net on the right side of your boat, and you will find fish," Jesus called to them.

They did so, and their net came up so full of fish, they could hardly pull it in. "Come and dine!" said Jesus. The disciples came ashore, and they shared a meal with him of bread and fish. No one asked him who he was, but they all knew he was Jesus.

Jesus Goes up to Heaven

The last time the disciples saw Jesus, he led them to the Mount of Olives. There he told them, "You must go back and wait in Jerusalem. Soon, the Holy Spirit will come to you. Then you will have the power to go out and spread my message."

He raised his hands and blessed them, and in that moment, he began to rise. The disciples watched as Jesus went up and up, until he disappeared inside a shining cloud. Then, with joy in their hearts, the disciples returned to Jerusalem and waited for the Holy Spirit to come to them.